CRIMCOMICS

DEVELOPMENTAL
AND LIFE-COURSE THEORIES

KRISTA S. GEHRING

WRITER

MICHAEL R. BATISTA

ARTIST

CHERYL L. WALLACE

LETTERER

New York   Oxford

OXFORD UNIVERSITY PRESS

DEDICATION

To Wilcox and Henderson,

Thank you for helping me navigate through one of the most difficult turning points in my life. If you've ever wondered if you have made an impact on any of your students' lives, you made a huge impact on mine.

—KRISTA S. GEHRING

Dedicated to Cheryl for continuing to crush it on letters despite the crazy last year.

—MICHAEL R. BATISTA

FOREWORD

How wildly exciting to learn that my work will be depicted in this fun comic book! It's terrific to be connected through this book with early-career students of criminology because you have the ideas that will take our field forward. If you can draw on the thinking that criminologists like Rob Sampson and I have done, to synthesize, integrate, and expand your own original thinking, then criminology will stay fresh and relevant as it always has been.

I would like to convey to you a bit about what research was like when I began working in criminology back in the 1980s as a student, at the time when I first wrote down my ideas about life-course-persistent and adolescence-limited offending that eventually appeared in print after a long struggle to get them published (Moffitt, 1993). The notion of developmental heterogeneity in the lives of criminal offenders is part of our lexicon today; it has become part of the vernacular of criminology, at least in some quarters. Why was the idea so mysterious and fascinating back then? As one example, the self-report method of measuring delinquency was fairly new and we were all just learning that official police data tap only the tip of the iceberg of offending behavior. As another example, the age-crime curve was fairly novel, and we were all scrambling to explain its shape. Why do so many people offend in their youth, and why can't some of them stop offending along with everyone else as they become adults? Imagine, as you can with the help of this comic book, a scene in a pub in Boston. Crisp autumn weather, the frisson

of promise that always comes with the beginning of the academic year, tall glasses of frothy beer on the table. My new boyfriend Avshalom Caspi, Rob Sampson, John Laub, and me, laughing and arguing and trying together to figure out what the age-crime curve is all about. Sessions like these were the inklings of what eventually grew into developmental life-course criminology, as accurately narrated in this comic book. Avshalom and I probably still owe Rob for the beers!

Quantitative trajectory modeling was not yet available as a tool to help us; Daniel Nagin brought that important tool to criminology in the 1990s. Magnetic resonance imaging (MRI) for studying neurological vulnerability was a decade away. Being able to work with measured genes to study gene-environment interplay was two decades away, and genome-wide methods were at least three decades away. The demographic shifts that brought the concept of "emerging adulthood" and the prolongation of adolescence years beyond high school had not been noticed yet by social scientists. Big-data methods to merge multiple nationwide administrative records for the same individual have vastly improved today, making it now possible to perform longitudinal developmental life-course research on multiple aspects of life among millions of people who represent whole nations. (I was able to merge Danish criminal court conviction records with psychiatric hospital records for 25,000 people in my PhD dissertation, but that was very unusual, and very cumbersome indeed). In the 1980s and 1990s, use of the internet by the public was far in the future, so naturally internet crime and the influence of social media on adolescent delinquency culture were in the future too. Despite our relative lack of information and tools, in my 1993 paper I ventured predictions about some of these phenomena, such as neurological vulnerability, gene-environment interplay, and the spillover from a criminal lifestyle to other aspects of life. It has since become possible for criminology to study them, and I recently wrote about interesting new avenues in research on life-course-persistent and adolescence-limited offending, such as the influence of internet crime (Moffitt, 2018). Maybe *you* will continue this research.

My own recent work has been exploring some of these new avenues. We were at last able to test the hypothesis that people whose antisocial behavior follows a life-course-persistent path have brain vulnerabilities, in a project led by University College London postdoc Christina Carlisi. In our Dunedin, New Zealand, birth cohort, structural MRI scans revealed that life-course-persistent antisocial participants, but not adolescence-limited participants, tended to have brains with a smaller surface area and a thinner cortex (Carlisi et al., 2020). The obvious shortcoming of this project was that we had not performed MRI scans prospectively during the participants' childhoods. However, MRI brain scanning wasn't possible in the 1970s, because the MRI came into practice in the late 1980s, and even then, it wasn't deemed a good idea to scan a child unless they had a suspected brain tumor. This lack of prospective scan data means that the brain structure differences we saw in our adult research participants could well be consequences of a persistent antisocial lifestyle, not a contributing cause. However, similar brain findings have been reported from contemporary studies of young children with aggressive conduct problems, suggesting that at least part of the brain differences we observed may have been present in childhood. Perhaps *you* will do the research to find out.

We also were at last able to test the longstanding hypothesis that young people whose antisocial behavior follows a life-course-persistent path began life with genetic vulnerabilities. In a project spearheaded by Duke University postdoc Jasmin Wertz, we studied genetic vulnerabilities known to interfere with young people's adjustment to school, which is the first institution of social control children encounter outside the family home. It so happens that the best genome-wide association study to date has pinned down genetic variants associated with educational attainment, and it is the best because of sample size: everyone who sends a saliva sample to 23andMe or Ancestry.com reports their highest degree, allowing the search for genetic variants associated with educational success in over a million individuals. In our UK and New Zealand cohorts born 20 years and 20,000 kilometers apart, life-course-persistent antisocial participants scored lower than adolescence-limited participants on the polygenic score that had been trained to predict success in education (Wertz et al. 2018). This finding helps to explain the oft-contested heritability of crime; it may actually be that what is inherited is characteristics that lead a child to experience school as humiliating and alienating, not a great place to build self-esteem. These characteristics could be cognitive skills, or non-cognitive skills such as self-control, both of which affect a child's ease of adjusting and learning in school. Young people who experience school as alienating tend to truncate their education and end up with limited alternatives to crime.

We developmental life-course researchers who work on longitudinal birth cohort studies must be jacks of all trades. We must work in many different topic areas to attract a resilient diverse funding portfolio to keep our cohort studies alive. Fortunately, each new wave of data collection multiplies the value of a cohort study exponentially by shedding light on new outcomes in a new stage of life. We cohort researchers scan the horizon for new measurement technologies our studies can adopt to improve knowledge about human development. Most important, we must scramble to become knowledgeable about new topic areas, in order to keep up with the members of our cohorts as they inexorably keep growing older and entering new life stages, encountering new social and health problems. They never stand still long enough to allow us to catch our breath. The story of my work trying to keep up with birth cohorts is told in a book from Harvard University Press (Belsky, Moffitt, et al.,

2020). Right now, I'm working on questions as varied as biological aging (Belsky, Caspi, et al., 2020) and mental health (Caspi et al., 2020), but developmental criminology is still my first true love. And it is lovely to see you reading this comic book to learn about it. I hope you find it as intellectually engaging as I do!

TERRIE MOFFITT
Duke University

Note: Part of this foreword is reprinted from Moffitt (2020).

REFERENCES

Belsky, D. W., Caspi, A., Arseneault, L., Baccarelli, A., Corcoran, D. L., Gao, X., Hannon, E., Harrington, H. L., Rassmussen, L. J. H., Houts, R., Huffman, K., Kraus, W. E., Kwon, D., Mill, J., Pieper, C., Prinz, J. A., Poulton, R., Schwartz, J., Sugden, K., Vokonas, P., Williams, B. S., & Moffitt, T. E. (2020). Quantification of the pace of biological aging in humans through a blood test: The DunedinPoAm DNA methylation algorithm. *eLife*. https://elifesciences.org/articles/54870

Belsky, J., Moffitt, T .E., Poulton, R., & Caspi, A. (2020). *The origins of you: How childhood shapes later life*. Harvard University Press.

Carlisi, C. O., Moffitt, T. E., Knodt, A. R., Harrington, H., Ireland, D., Melzer, T. R., Poulton, R., Ramrakha, S., Caspi, A., Hariri, A. R., & Viding, E. (2020). Associations between life-course-persistent antisocial behavior and brain structure in a longitudinal birth cohort. *Lancet-Psychiatry*, 7(3), 245–253. https//doi.org/10.1016/S2215-0366(20)30002-X

Caspi, A., Houts, R. M., Ambler, A., Danese, A., Elliott, M. L., Hariri, A., Harrington, H., Hogan, S., Poulton, R., Ramrakha, S., Hartmann Rasmussen, L. J., Reuben, A., Richmond-Rakerd, L., Sugden, K., Wertz, J., Williams, B. S., & Moffitt, T. E.

(2020). Longitudinal assessment of mental disorders and comorbidities across four decades among participants in the Dunedin birth cohort Study. *JAMA-Network Open*, 3(4), e203221. https://jamanetwork.com/journals/jamanetworkopen/fullarticle/2764602

Moffitt, T. E. (1993). "Life-course-persistent" and "adolescence-limited" antisocial behavior: A developmental taxonomy. *Psychological Review*, 100, 674–701.

Moffitt, T. E. (2018). Male antisocial behavior in adolescence and beyond. *Nature Human Behaviour*, 2, 177–186. https//doi.org/10.1038/s41562-018-0309-4

Moffitt, T. E. (2020). Innovations in life-court crime research. *Journal of Developmental and Life-Course Criminology*, 6, 251–266. https://link.springer.com/article/10.1007/s40865-020-00153-5

Wertz, J., Caspi, A., Belsky, D. W., Beckley, A. L., Arseneault, L., Barnes, J. C., Corcoran, D. L., Hogan, S., Houts, R., Morgan, N., Odgers, C. L., Prinz, J., Sugden, K., Williams, B. S., Poulton, R., & Moffitt, T. E. (2018). Genetics and crime: Integrating new genomic discoveries into psychological research about antisocial behavior: Replicated evidence from two birth cohorts. *Psychological Science*, 29(5), 791–803. https//doi.org/10.1177/0956797617744542

PREFACE

I think this issue best exemplifies one of the reasons why I love theory so much. When I begin my research, I am always astounded at how interconnected many theorists are and how this, among other things, impacts how they think about crime. This issue in particular illustrates not only development and life-course theories, but how these scholars experienced significant events, "turning points" if you will, that led them down a particular trajectory regarding their scholarship. This is the reason there is so much narrative about these theorists in this issue, because quite frankly, it's fascinating, especially when you conduct a thought exercise of "what ifs."

For example, what if Travis Hirschi received permission to use Sheldon and Eleanor Glueck's data for his research? It is likely he would not have formulated his social bond theory and his research would have gone in a different direction. Furthermore, it would have either diminished or outright eliminated John Laub's later discovery of the Glueck data in the Harvard Law Library sub-basement.

What if the State University of New York at Albany had not decided to create a premier criminal justice program in the early 1980s? Travis Hirschi wouldn't have taught there, Michael Gottfredson might not have reunited with him as a graduate student, and Robert Sampson and John Laub likely would have never met as graduate students in that program. It's likely that these and other individuals in those early cohorts would not have gone on to make such tremendous contributions to the discipline.

What if Terrie Moffitt and her fellow doctoral student friends hadn't gotten the crazy idea of jumping out of an airplane prior to their dissertation defense? Perhaps she wouldn't have been a captive audience for Phil Silva for him to convince her to get involved with the Dunedin Study. Perhaps she would have continued on making great scholarly contributions, but she would have likely never developed her developmental taxonomy.

What if John Laub didn't get that fellowship with the Radcliffe Institute? What if he

chose a different focus for his project? What if he didn't mention the Glueck data to that librarian? It's likely he would have gone on to write about other topics, but he would have never developed the age-graded theory with Robert Sampson. If these things had not happened, it's possible that data could still be moldering in that sub-basement today.

I put forth these hypothetical scenarios to illustrate how much time and place matters, not only for theories, but for theorists as well. At any point in time, an individual can experience a "turning point" that sets them on a new trajectory during their life course. This concept is reflected in the theories you are about to learn, as for some, "turning points" may impact their entry into or desistence from crime just as the "turning points" for these theorists influenced their path into a particular area of criminological thought.

As with any book project, *CrimComics* consumed much time and effort, perhaps more so than a traditional textbook. Thinking about theory—and, in particular, trying to design a work that best conveys the theories in a visual medium—is fun. Still, with busy lives, finding the space in one's day to carefully research, write, illustrate, ink, and letter the pages of this work is a source of some stress. We were fortunate, however, to have had an amazing amount of support during these times from family, friends, and Oxford University Press. We also want to acknowledge the talents of Cheryl Wallace. Cheryl's flair for lettering allowed us to get our ideas across to the readers.

The support of these and so many other individuals has made creating *CrimComics* possible and a rewarding experience for us. We would like to thank the following reviewers: Elizabeth B. Perkins, Morehead State University; Viviana Andreescu, University of Louisville; Suman Kakar, Florida International University; Ellen G. Cohn, Florida International University. We hope that this and other issues of *CrimComics* will inspire in your students a passion to learn criminological theory.

Developmental and Life-Course Theories

CONTINUITY AND CHANGE ARE HALLMARK CHARACTERISTICS OF
DEVELOPMENTAL THEORIES AND *LIFE-COURSE THEORIES*
IN CRIMINOLOGY.

DEVELOPMENTAL THEORIES FOCUS ON A DEVELOPMENTAL PROCESS
IN WHICH A PERSON PASSES THROUGH PREDICTABLE STAGES
DURING HIS OR HER LIFETIME.

THAT IS, A PERSON'S OFFENDING BEHAVIOR UNFOLDS IN
EXPECTED WAYS.

LIFE-COURSE THEORIES DO NOT SUGGEST THAT BEHAVIOR
IS THAT EASILY PREDICTED.

WHILE THERE MAY BE ELEMENTS THAT INCREASE OR DECREASE
THE LIKELIHOOD OF OFFENDING BEHAVIOR, THERE ARE ALSO
UNPREDICTABLE EVENTS THAT MAY IMPACT WHETHER A PERSON
STOPS COMMITTING CRIME.

BOTH TYPES OF THEORIES FOCUS ON DETERMINING THE ONSET,
PERSISTENCE, AND DESISTENCE OF OFFENDING, AS WELL AS THE
PATHWAY OR SEQUENCE OF EVENTS THAT LEAD PEOPLE
INTO AND OUT OF CRIME.

PRIOR TO THESE TYPES OF THEORIES, CRIMINOLOGICAL THEORIES HAD BEEN DEVELOPED BY STUDYING SAMPLES OF ADOLESCENTS (MAINLY MALES).

UNRAVELING DELINQUENCY

Juvenile Delinquency and Urban Areas

Delinquency and Opportunity

DELINQUENT BOYS

Causes of Delinquency

DELINQUENCY AND DRIFT

EVENTS IN CHILDHOOD WERE ALL BUT IGNORED BY THESE THEORIES, AND THIS IS EVIDENCED IN THE TITLES OF THEORISTS' PUBLISHED WORKS.

THIS IMPLIED THAT DELINQUENCY IS A "TEENAGE PROBLEM," AND THAT CHILDREN ARE BLANK SLATES UNTIL THEY REACH ADOLESCENCE.

HOWEVER, RESEARCH EMERGED THAT ILLUSTRATED THAT ANTISOCIAL BEHAVIOR IN CHILDHOOD WAS RELATED TO DELINQUENCY IN ADOLESCENCE AND CRIMINAL BEHAVIOR IN ADULTHOOD.

THE FOCUS ON ADOLESCENCE HAD COMPLETELY MISSED A STAGE OF DEVELOPMENT, CHILDHOOD, THAT HAD AN IMPACT ON THE DEVELOPMENT OF LATER ANTISOCIAL BEHAVIOR.

I'M SO PROUD OF YOU, SON. YOU REALLY TURNED YOUR LIFE AROUND!

THE FOCUS ON ADOLESCENCE HAD ALSO FAILED TO EXPLAIN OFFENDING DURING ADULTHOOD, AND WHEN AND IF IT DECREASED OR STOPPED.

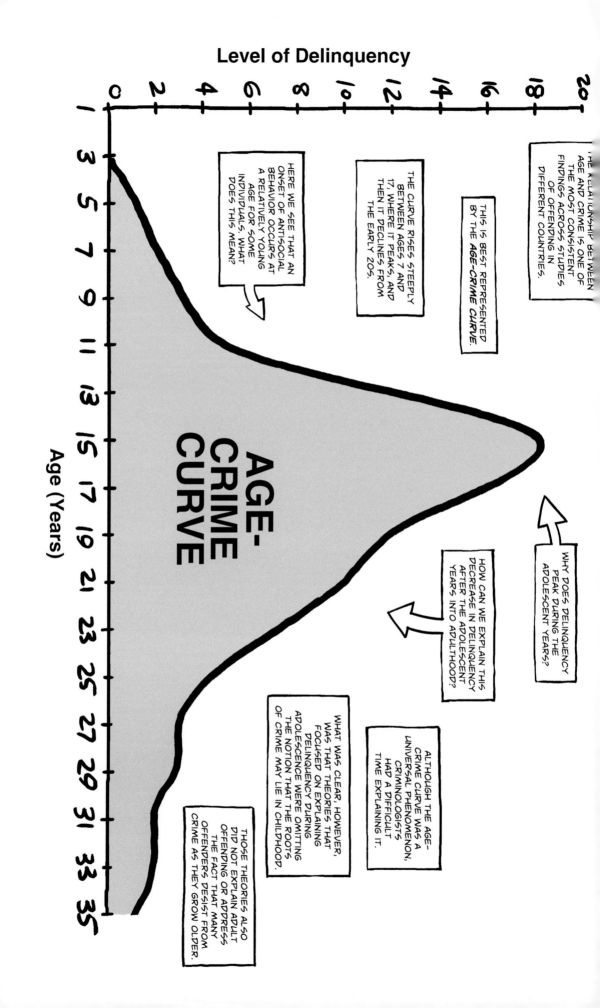

THE DEVELOPMENT OF LIFE-COURSE AND DEVELOPMENTAL THEORIES HAS QUITE AN INTERESTING BACKSTORY.

THE GENESIS OF THESE THEORIES MIRRORS THE ASSUMPTIONS THAT ARE PUT FORTH IN LIFE-COURSE CRIMINOLOGY ITSELF: THAT THERE ARE UNPREDICTABLE EVENTS THAT OCCUR THAT MAY IMPACT A PERSON'S TRAJECTORY THROUGH LIFE.

THE CRIMINAL JUSTICE DEPARTMENT AT THE STATE UNIVERSITY OF NEW YORK AT ALBANY IN THE LATE 1970S WAS AN INTELLECTUAL POWERHOUSE.

THE FACULTY WHO WERE RECRUITED TO TEACH THERE WERE CURRENT GIANTS IN THE FIELDS OF CRIMINOLOGY AND CRIMINAL JUSTICE. THERE WERE ALSO EXCEPTIONAL GRADUATE STUDENTS THERE WHO LATER WENT ON TO SHAPE THE FIELD.

ROBERT SAMPSON* WAS ONE OF THESE GRADUATE STUDENTS. HE AND MANY OTHERS WERE ABLE TO TAKE A SEMINAR TAUGHT BY TRAVIS HIRSCHI.*

I'M ASSUMING YOU ALL ARE FAMILIAR WITH THE WORKS OF SHELDON AND ELEANOR GLUECK?

Unraveling Juvenile Delinquency

THE GLUECKS WERE CRIMINOLOGISTS AND RESEARCHERS AT HARVARD LAW SCHOOL.

ONE OF THEIR MOST NOTABLE STUDIES INVOLVED 500 DELINQUENT BOYS FROM MASSACHUSETTS TRAINING SCHOOLS MATCHED WITH 500 NON-DELINQUENT BOYS FROM BOSTON PUBLIC SCHOOLS.

BY FOLLOWING THESE BOYS OVER TIME, UNTIL ABOUT AGE 32, THEY FOUND THAT DELINQUENCY WAS THE RESULT OF A COMBINATION OF VARIOUS BIOLOGICAL, TEMPERAMENTAL, INTELLECTUAL, AND SOCIO-CULTURAL (ESPECIALLY FAMILY) RISK FACTORS.

THEY ALSO FOUND THAT JUVENILE DELINQUENT CAREERS TENDED TO LEAD TO ADULT CRIMINAL CAREERS.

*MORE ON ROBERT SAMPSON IN CRIMCOMICS: SOCIAL DISORGANIZATION THEORY AND TRAVIS HIRSCHI IN CRIMCOMICS: SOCIAL CONTROL THEORIES!

I WROTE TO THE GLUECKS AND ASKED THEM IF I COULD USE THEIR DATA FOR MY DISSERTATION.

THEY DECLINED... BUT I THINK THINGS WORKED OUT WELL FOR ME IN SPITE OF THAT.

THE DEPARTMENT ALSO HOUSED THE CENTER FOR CRIMINAL JUSTICE RESEARCH. THIS WAS A PLACE WHERE GRADUATE STUDENTS CONGREGATED AND WORKED TOGETHER ON RESEARCH PROJECTS WITH FACULTY MEMBERS.

JOHN LAUB, A GRADUATE STUDENT AT THAT TIME.

HEY, ROB! FINISHED WITH CLASS?

MICHAEL GOTTFREDSON,* FORMER GRADUATE STUDENT, CURRENT ASSISTANT PROFESSOR AND DIRECTOR OF THE CENTER AT THAT TIME.

YES. EVERY TIME I LEAVE HIRSCHI'S CLASS I FEEL LIKE MY HEAD IS GOING TO EXPLODE.

HE HAS THAT EFFECT ON PEOPLE. REMEMBER, I HAD HIM AS AN UNDERGRADUATE STUDENT AT UC-DAVIS BEFORE I TOOK HIM AS A GRADUATE STUDENT HERE.

AND NOW YOU ARE ON THE FACULTY AND COLLEAGUES WITH HIM. THAT'S SO COOL.

HEY, ROB, WE SHOULD WRITE A "QUICK AND DIRTY" PAPER SOON. WE HAVEN'T WRITTEN ANYTHING TOGETHER YET.

SURE, JOHN-- THAT'D BE GREAT. JUST HIT ME UP WHEN YOU HAVE AN IDEA OR SOMETHING.

EVENTUALLY THESE STUDENTS AND THEIR MENTORS SCATTERED TO THE WIND AND TOOK UP POSITIONS AT OTHER UNIVERSITIES...

*CHECK OUT MICHAEL GOTTFREDSON IN CRIMCOMICS: SOCIAL CONTROL THEORIES!

THE NEXT DAY.

TERRIE! WHAT HAPPENED? ARE YOU ALL RIGHT?

YES, I'M FINE, SARNOFF. JUST A LITTLE SKY-DIVING ACCIDENT. A GROUP OF US--

A GROUP OF YOU DID THIS? IS ANYONE ELSE HURT?

WELL...KATHY DISLOCATED BOTH OF HER SHOULDERS...

SO THAT'S WHY HARDLY ANYONE IS IN HERE WORKING?

EXCUSE ME, PHIL. I NEED TO MAKE SOME PHONE CALLS.

TERRIE, THIS IS *PHIL SILVA*. HE IS VISITING FROM NEW ZEALAND AND IS THE CURRENT DIRECTOR OF THE *DUNEDIN MULTIDISCIPLINARY HEALTH AND DEVELOP-MENT STUDY* (AKA THE DUNEDIN STUDY).

CAN YOU CHAT WITH HIM WHILE I GET A HANDLE ON THIS SKYDIVING DEBACLE?

OH! WELL, WELCOME TO CALIFORNIA! WHAT BRINGS YOU HERE?

THANK YOU! I'M TRAVELING AROUND THE COUNTRY GETTING RESEARCH IDEAS ABOUT WHAT WE COULD LOOK AT WITH THE STUDY DATA.

I'M ALSO ACTING AS A SORT OF TALENT SCOUT TO SEE IF I CAN GET YOUNG RESEARCHERS TO COME AND DO RESEARCH IN NEW ZEALAND...

WOULD YOU BE INTEREST- ED?

OH, I DON'T KNOW. I NEED TO DEFEND MY DISSERTATION, AND I HAD PLANNED TO LOOK FOR A FACULTY POSITION AFTER I GRADUATED.

AND TRAVELING TO ANOTHER COUNTRY WASN'T PART OF MY PLANS...

HOURS LATER.

YOU COULD COMBINE YOUR SCIENTIFIC INTERESTS OF EXAMINING LONGITUDINAL COHORT DATA, THE NEUROPSYCHOLOGICAL STUDY OF BRAIN FUNCTION, AND THE QUESTION OF WHY PEOPLE ENGAGE IN CRIME.

WE HAVE VARIABLES IN THE DATA THAT MEASURE ALL OF THAT.

SEVERAL MORE HOURS LATER.

NEW ZEALAND IS SUCH A BEAUTIFUL PLACE!

AN HOUR AFTER THAT.

PHIL! MY APOLOGIES THAT I LEFT YOU FOR SO LONG!

NOT TO WORRY! I BELIEVE I'VE FINALLY CONVINCED HER TO COME AND WORK ON THE DUNEDIN STUDY...

THAT IS AN EXCELLENT OPPORTUNITY, TERRIE. JUST MAKE SURE THAT THE PLANE LANDS IN NEW ZEALAND BEFORE YOU JUMP OUT OF IT, OKAY?

IN 1984, MOFFITT RECEIVED A GRANT FROM THE NATIONAL INSTITUTE OF MENTAL HEALTH TO TRAVEL TO NEW ZEALAND TO RESEARCH WHETHER NEUROPSYCHOLOGICAL DEFICITS IN PRE-ADOLESCENTS COULD PREDICT LATER DELINQUENCY AND VIOLENCE IN ADOLESCENCE.

HAVE YOU EVER ATTACKED ANYONE WITH A WEAPON, SUCH AS A KNIFE, OR BEAT THEM WITH A STICK?

NAH... WELL, JUST CATHOLICS.

FOR TWO YEARS SHE ADMINISTERED NEUROPSYCHOLOGICA ASSESSMENTS TO 1,000 13-YEAR-OLDS AND INTERVIEWED THEM ABOUT THEIR SELF-REPORTED DELINQUENCY.

IN 1985, GOTTFREDSON WAS REUNITED WITH HIRSCHI AT THE UNIVERSITY OF ARIZONA WHEN HE ACQUIRED AN ASSISTANT PROFESSOR POSITION THERE (HIRSCHI HAD BEEN THERE SINCE 1981).

AT THAT SAME TIME, SAMPSON WAS AN ASSISTANT PROFESSOR IN THE SOCIOLOGY DEPARTMENT AT THE UNIVERSITY OF ILLINOIS AT URBANA-CHAMPAIGN...

...AND LAUB WAS AN ASSOCIATE PROFESSOR IN THE COLLEGE OF CRIMINAL JUSTICE AT NORTHEASTERN UNIVERSITY.

LAUB WAS ALSO A VISITING FELLOW AT THE CENTER FOR CRIMINAL JUSTICE AT HARVARD LAW SCHOOL.

HE HAD JUST PUBLISHED THE BOOK *CRIMINOLOGY IN THE MAKING* (1983) IN WHICH HE INTERVIEWED NINE OF THE MOST SIGNIFICANT FIGURES IN CRIMINOLOGY AT THE TIME WHO HAD CONTRIBUTED TO THE FIELD BETWEEN 1930 AND 1960.

NOW, AS A FELLOW, HE NEEDED TO FIND ANOTHER RESEARCH TOPIC.

LUCKILY, HIS FELLOWSHIP PROVIDED HIM WITH ACCESS TO ALL THE LIBRARIES AT HARVARD UNIVERSITY.

HE WAS TOYING WITH THE IDEA OF GOING BACK TO AN EARLIER PERIOD OF CRIMINOLOGY--1900 TO 1930--AND LEARNING MORE ABOUT THE FOUNDATIONS OF AMERICAN CRIMINOLOGY.

HE THOUGHT HE'D START WITH RESEARCHING THE GLUECKS.

EXCUSE ME? DO YOU HAPPEN TO HAVE ANY OF SHELDON AND ELEANOR GLUECKS' MATERIALS?

Quiet Please

CIRCULATION

THE ARTICLES GOTTFREDSON AND HIRSCHI WROTE DEVELOPED INTO SOMETHING MUCH LARGER.

SO, THIS IS WHAT WE KNOW: THE AGE-CRIME CURVE IS INVARIANT, AND CRIME DECLINES WITH AGE.

THESE BEHAVIORS BEGIN EARLY IN LIFE, NOT JUST DURING ADOLESCENCE.

SO, ALL THE THEORIES THAT HAVE FOCUSED PRIMARILY ON ADOLESCENCE MAY IN FACT BE INADEQUATE.

BEGINNING IN CHILDHOOD IS THE KEY.

Michael R. Gottfredson and Travis Hirschi

A GENERAL THEORY OF CRIME

IN 1990, GOTTFREDSON AND HIRSCHI PUBLISHED *A GENERAL THEORY OF CRIME*. IN IT, THEY PROPOSED *SELF-CONTROL THEORY*. GOTTFREDSON AND HIRSCHI SETTLED ON THE CONCEPT OF *SELF-CONTROL* IN ORDER TO DEVELOP A GENERAL THEORY THAT IDENTIFIED THE TENDENCY TO IGNORE COSTS IN FAVOR OF SHORT-TERM BENEFITS. SELF-CONTROL IS THE RESTRAINT THAT ALLOWS PEOPLE TO RESIST CRIME AND OTHER SHORT-TERM GRATIFICATION. PEOPLE WITH LOW SELF-CONTROL TEND TO BE "IMPULSIVE, INSENSITIVE, PHYSICAL (AS OPPOSED TO MENTAL), RISK-TAKING, SHORT-SIGHTED, AND NON-VERBAL."

GOTTFREDSON AND HIRSCHI HYPOTHESIZED THAT LOW SELF-CONTROL IS THE RESULT OF INEFFECTIVE PARENTING. INEFFECTIVE PARENTING OCCURS WHEN PARENTS DO NOT MONITOR, RECOGNIZE, AND PUNISH DEVIANT BEHAVIOR.

ACCORDING TO GOTTFREDSON AND HIRSCHI, SELF-CONTROL STABILIZES BY THE TIME THE CHILD REACHES THE AGE OF EIGHT. THEREFORE, THE LEVEL OF SELF-CONTROL IS STABLE OVER THE LIFE COURSE AND WILL AFFECT VIRTUALLY EVERY ASPECT OF A PERSON'S LIFE. THIS IS A THEORY THAT EXPLAINED *CONTINUITY* IN OFFENDING.

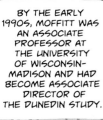

BY THE EARLY 1990S, MOFFITT WAS AN ASSOCIATE PROFESSOR AT THE UNIVERSITY OF WISCONSIN-MADISON AND HAD BECOME ASSOCIATE DIRECTOR OF THE DUNEDIN STUDY.

SHE WAS PUBLISHING A LOT OF ARTICLES USING THE DATA.

HOWEVER, SOMETHING EMERGED IN THE DATA THAT SHE COULDN'T EXPLAIN.

SO, THE 13-YEAR-OLDS WITH NEUROPSYCHOLOGICAL DEFICITS ARE ALREADY MORE INVOLVED IN MINOR DELINQUENCY BY AGE 13 THAN THEIR PEERS.

I WOULD ASSUME THAT WHEN I FOLLOW UP WITH THE COHORT AT AGES 15 AND 18, THE CORRELATION BETWEEN THESE DEFICITS AND CRIME WILL BECOME STRONGER.

I DON'T UNDERSTAND. AS MORE YOUTH ARE ENGAGING IN DELINQUENCY AT AGES 15 AND 18, THE CORRELATIONS BETWEEN THE RISK FACTORS AND DELINQUENCY BECOME WEAKER AND WEAKER.

NOW I HAVE NO FINDINGS TO PUBLISH AT ALL.

THIS IS NOT WHAT I EXPECTED.

BUT...WHY WERE RISK FACTORS IMPORTANT FOR KIDS WHOSE DELINQUENCY BEGAN BEFORE ADOLESCENCE BUT NOT FOR KIDS WHOSE DELINQUENCY BEGAN AT MID-ADOLESCENCE?

IN THE EARLY 1990S, SAMPSON AND LAUB WERE STILL WORKING WITH THE GLUECK DATA. THEY RECEIVED A GRANT FROM THE NATIONAL INSTITUTE OF JUSTICE TO CODE AND ANALYZE THE GLUECKS' LONGITUDINAL DATA COLLECTED OVER THREE WAVES.

YOU KNOW, I'M NOT CONVINCED BY MIKE AND TRAVIS'S GENERAL THEORY OF CRIME, THAT PARENTING PRACTICES AND TEMPERAMENT ARE ALL WE NEED TO KNOW TO UNDERSTAND PATTERNS IN ADULT OFFENDING.

THEY ARE ESSENTIALLY SAYING THAT ONLY CONTINUITY IN OFFENDING EXISTS.

I KNOW-- THERE IS SO MUCH DATA HERE THAT WE CAN EXAMINE CRIME AND DEVIANCE IN CHILDHOOD, ADOLESCENCE, AND ADULTHOOD THAT LOOKS AT WHETHER CONTINUITY AND CHANGE OVER THE LIFE COURSE HAPPENS.

THE MORE I LOOK AT THIS, THE MORE I SEE THAT SOME INDIVIDUALS CHANGE IN THEIR LIFETIMES, ESPECIALLY WHEN CERTAIN EVENTS HAPPEN.

I MEAN, IT LOOKS LIKE SOME OF THESE SUBJECTS HAVE THINGS HAPPEN TO THEM THAT SEND THEM ON A COMPLETELY DIFFERENT TRAJECTORY AWAY FROM CRIME.

CAUSES of DELINQUENCY

Travis Hirschi

IT WOULD BE GREAT IF WE COULD FIND SOME THEORETICAL FRAMEWORK TO BUILD THESE IDEAS UPON.

THIS IS SO IRONIC,* BUT I THINK I MAY HAVE FOUND IT...

*IT SHOULD BE NOTED THAT THE GLUECK DATA THAT WAS DENIED TO HIRSCHI WAS NOW BEING USED BY HIS FORMER DOCTORAL STUDENTS, AND THEY USED HIS SOCIAL BOND THEORY AS A FRAMEWORK TO DEVELOP THEIR LIFE-COURSE THEORY WHILE HIRSCHI HAD ABANDONED THAT SAME THEORY TO DEVELOP SELF-CONTROL THEORY WITH GOTTFREDSON.

IN 1993, MOFFITT PUBLISHED HER SEMINAL WORK THAT EXPLAINED WHAT SHE HAD INITIALLY FOUND SO CONFUSING IN HER DATA. IN THIS PUBLICATION, SHE DETAILS HER **DEVELOPMENTAL TAXONOMY** (SOMETIMES CALLED **DUAL TAXONOMY THEORY**) IN WHICH SHE PROPOSED THAT THE AGE-CRIME CURVE CONSISTS OF TWO QUALITATIVELY DISTINCT GROUPS OF OFFENDERS.

Adolescence-Limited and Life-Course-Persistent Antisocial Behavior: A Developmental Taxonomy

Terrie E. Moffitt

HER THEORY PROPOSED THAT OFFENDING IS MARKED BY CONTINUITY OR CHANGE.

TONY, STOP IT! STOP CRYING RIGHT NOW.

EACH GROUP HAS ITS OWN ETIOLOGICAL PATH INTO AND OUT OF DELINQUENT AND CRIMINAL BEHAVIOR. **LIFE-COURSE-PERSISTENT (LCP)** OFFENDERS BEGIN ANTISOCIAL BEHAVIOR AT AN EARLY AGE, AND THEIR ANTISOCIAL BEHAVIOR CONTINUES ACROSS THE LIFE COURSE. THEY ARE A SMALL GROUP OF INDIVIDUALS BUT ACCOUNT FOR A LARGE PORTION OF CRIMES.

THE CAUSE OF THEIR ANTISOCIAL BEHAVIOR IS FOUND IN EARLY CHILDHOOD AND IS DUE TO **NEUROPSYCHOLOGICAL DEFICITS**. THESE DEFICITS INCLUDE POOR VERBAL AND EXECUTIVE FUNCTIONS, SUCH AS ISSUES WITH PROBLEM SOLVING, MEMORY, INATTENTION, AND IMPULSIVITY.

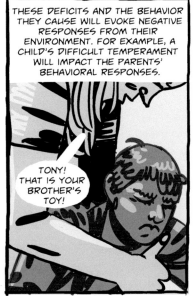

THESE DEFICITS AND THE BEHAVIOR THEY CAUSE WILL EVOKE NEGATIVE RESPONSES FROM THEIR ENVIRONMENT. FOR EXAMPLE, A CHILD'S DIFFICULT TEMPERAMENT WILL IMPACT THE PARENTS' BEHAVIORAL RESPONSES.

TONY! THAT IS YOUR BROTHER'S TOY!

TONY, WHY DON'T YOU MIND ME WHEN I TELL YOU NOT TO DO SOMETHING?

THE CHALLENGE OF COPING WITH A DIFFICULT CHILD EVOKES A CHAIN OF FAILED CHILD-PARENT INTERACTIONS.

AS THESE INDIVIDUALS AGE, THEIR ACTIONS TEND TO ESCALATE IN SEVERITY.

YOU WANT A DIME OR A QUARTER BAG?

THE NEGATIVE REACTIONS THE INDIVIDUAL EVOKES FROM THE ENVIRONMENT CHARACTERIZE MANY INTERACTIONS IN ALL ASPECTS OF THE PERSON'S LIFE.

TO THE PRINCIPAL'S OFFICE, YOUNG MAN.

WHATEVER--I'M DONE WITH THIS PLACE.

THESE INTERACTIONS CAUSE THE CONTINUITY OF LCP OFFENDERS' BEHAVIORS, AS THEY GENERATE *CUMULATIVE CONTINUITY*. CUMULATIVE CONTINUITY IS THE PROCESS BY WHICH A PERSON'S ACTIONS PRODUCE RESULTS THAT ACCUMULATE OVER TIME AND MOVE ALONG SPECIFIC LIFE TRAJECTORIES.

LCP OFFENDERS CONTINUE THEIR OFFENDING BEHAVIOR WELL INTO ADULTHOOD.

THIS IS A RESULT OF *CONTEMPORARY CONTINUITY*.

THAT IS, THE LCP OFFENDER CARRIES INTO ADULTHOOD THE SAME UNDERLYING COLLECTION OF TRAITS THAT GOT HIM OR HER INTO TROUBLE AS A CHILD, SUCH AS IRRITABILITY, LOW SELF-CONTROL, AND LOW COGNITIVE ABILITY.

THEREFORE, LCP OFFENDING BEHAVIOR IS MARKED BY CONTINUITY.

GET HIM!

THE OTHER GROUP OF OFFENDERS IN MOFFITT'S THEORY DO NOT EXHIBIT ANTISOCIAL BEHAVIOR IN CHILDHOOD.

MOMMY, CAN WE GO SEE THE MONKEYS?

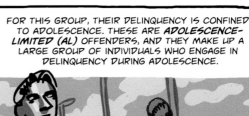

FOR THIS GROUP, THEIR DELINQUENCY IS CONFINED TO ADOLESCENCE. THESE ARE *ADOLESCENCE-LIMITED (AL)* OFFENDERS, AND THEY MAKE UP A LARGE GROUP OF INDIVIDUALS WHO ENGAGE IN DELINQUENCY DURING ADOLESCENCE.

HEY, CHRIS, YOU GOING TO SENIOR KEGS AT DEER CREEK THIS WEEKEND?

I'LL DEFINITELY BE THERE. JUST HAVE TO FIGURE OUT HOW TO GET OUT OF THE HOUSE.

LATER THAT NIGHT.

CHRIS-TOPHER? WHERE ARE YOU GOING?

DON'T THINK YOU ARE GOING TO ANY OF THOSE "KEGGERS" THIS WEEKEND.

GOSH, MOM! WHY CAN'T YOU LET ME JUST LIVE MY LIFE?

AL OFFENDERS ENGAGE IN DELINQUENCY IN ORDER TO OVERCOME THE *MATURITY GAP*.

CHRISTOPHER! COME BACK HERE!

COME BACK HERE OR YOU ARE GROUNDED!

SLAM

THAT IS, WHILE THEIR BODIES HAVE MATURED BIOLOGICALLY, THEY ARE NOT TREATED LIKE ADULTS.

DUDE, YOUR MOM IS LETTING YOU GO?

I DON'T CARE WHAT MY MOM SAYS--I WISH SHE'D STOP TREATING ME LIKE A BABY AND LET ME MAKE MY OWN DECISIONS.

SINCE AL OFFENDERS HAVE NOT HAD MUCH EXPERIENCE IN HOW TO BEHAVE BADLY, THEY LOOK TO OTHERS TO IMITATE.

C-DAWG, YOU MADE IT.

'SUP TONY?

WE WERE JUST GOING TO SHOOT SOME BEERS-- YOU IN?

AL OFFENDERS ENGAGE IN *SOCIAL MIMICRY* AND IMITATE THE BEHAVIOR OF THEIR LCP PEERS.

THESE ACTS OF DELINQUENCY SHOW *AUTONOMY* AND THUS REINFORCE AL OFFENDERS' BEHAVIOR.

ONCE AL OFFENDERS REACH ADULTHOOD, THE MATURITY GAP CLOSES AND THE NEED TO ENGAGE IN CRIME DISAPPEARS. FOR THEM, THE COSTS OF COMMITTING CRIME ARE TOO HIGH NOW. THEREFORE, AL OFFENDERS' OFFENDING BEHAVIOR IS MARKED BY CHANGE.

1993 WAS ALSO THE YEAR THAT SAMPSON AND LAUB PUBLISHED THEIR SEMINAL WORK, *CRIME IN THE MAKING*. IN IT, THEY PROPOSED AN **AGE-GRADED THEORY** OF INFORMAL SOCIAL CONTROL TO EXPLAIN CRIME AND DEVIANCE OVER THE LIFE COURSE.

THEIR THEORY PROPOSED THAT OFFENDING IS MARKED BY CONTINUITY AND CHANGE.

SAMPSON AND LAUB APPLIED HIRSCHI'S **SOCIAL BOND THEORY** TO THE GLUECK DATA.

THEY PROPOSED THAT SOCIAL BONDS ARE AGE-GRADED. THAT IS, SOCIAL BONDS VARY THROUGHOUT LIFE.

FOR EXAMPLE, BONDS TO FAMILY AND SCHOOL ARE IMPORTANT IN CHILDHOOD AND ADOLESCENCE.

MAN, MY PARENTS DON'T CARE ABOUT ME. I HAVEN'T BEEN HOME IN THREE DAYS--YOU THINK THEY NOTICE?

IF THOSE BONDS ARE WEAK, IT EXPLAINS CONTINUITY IN OFFENDING.

THE ROLE OF CONTINUITY IN PROBLEM BEHAVIOR EXTENDS FROM YOUTH INTO ADULTHOOD AND OCCURS IN A VARIETY OF FORMS, SUCH AS CRIME, SUBSTANCE ABUSE, DIVORCE, AND UNEMPLOYMENT.

YO, JOHNNY. I HEAR IT'S YOUR BIRTHDAY NEXT WEEK.

THEY GOING TO SEND YOU TO THE BIG HOUSE CUZ YOU'RE TURNING 18?

SEVERAL YEARS LATER.

IMPORTANT SOCIAL BONDS CHANGE WHEN ONE ENTERS INTO ADULTHOOD.

THE BONDS WITH PARENTS AND SCHOOL ARE NOT AS IMPORTANT, WHILE OTHER INSTITUTIONS OF INFORMAL SOCIAL CONTROL, LIKE EMPLOYMENT OR MARRIAGE, ARE.

HEY GUY--WE ARE CLOSING IN FIVE MINUTES. WRAP IT UP, OKAY?

SAMPSON AND LAUB PROPOSE THAT THE LACK OF ADEQUATE SOCIAL BONDS IN THE TRANSITION TO YOUNG ADULTHOOD EXPLAINS CRIMINAL BEHAVIOR CONTINUING INTO ADULTHOOD.

THEREFORE, WEAK OR NONEXISTENT SOCIAL BONDS THROUGHOUT THE LIFE COURSE HAVE A DIRECT IMPACT ON BEHAVIOR.

GIVE ME ALL THE MONEY AND NO ONE GETS HURT!

IN AN ALTERNATE REALITY...

SAMPSON AND LAUB ALSO PROPOSE THAT SALIENT LIFE EVENTS CAN IMPACT TRAJECTORIES IN ADULTHOOD.

HEY... HEY, IS THAT YOU, JOHN?

JEEZ, I HAVEN'T SEEN YOU SINCE HIGH SCHOOL! HOW'VE YOU BEEN?

AH...I JUST GOT OUT OF THE JOINT.

WHAT ARE YOU GOING TO DO?

I DON'T KNOW. MY OPTIONS ARE PRETTY LIMITED RIGHT NOW.

"LISTEN, HOW ABOUT YOU COME WORK FOR ME? I'VE GOT A RESTAURANT, AND WE ARE ALWAYS LOOKING FOR HELP."

INDIVIDUALS CAN EXPERIENCE **TURNING POINTS** IN THEIR LIVES, LIKE LEGITIMATE EMPLOYMENT, A STABLE MARRIAGE, OR ENTERING THE MILITARY.

THESE LIFE EVENTS COULD HAPPEN AT ANY TIME, AND THEY EXPLAIN DESISTENCE OF CRIMINAL BEHAVIOR.

THAT IS, THESE LIFE EVENTS CAN EXPLAIN CHANGE* IN OFFENDING.

*IN THEIR WORK SHARED BEGINNINGS, DIVERGENT LIVES (2003), LAUB AND SAMPSON DISCUSSED HOW CHANGE IS ALSO DUE TO **HUMAN AGENCY**; THAT IS, IT IS WILLED TO A CERTAIN EXTENT.

SINCE THESE THEORIES FOCUS ON CHILDHOOD AS THE ORIGIN OF SERIOUS PERSISTENT OFFENDING, THERE ARE DIRECT POLICY IMPLICATIONS.

IDEAS CAUSE REACTIONS.

BASED ON THESE THEORIES, *EARLY INTERVENTION PROGRAMS* ARE THE MOST EFFECTIVE WAYS OF PREVENTING CRIMES.

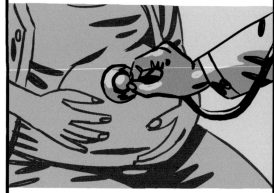

FOR EXAMPLE, MOTHERS WHO RECEIVE PROPER PRENATAL CARE AND WHO AVOID BEHAVIORS THAT PUT FETAL DEVELOPMENT AT RISK (E.G., DRUG USE, ALCOHOL CONSUMPTION, SMOKING) CAN REDUCE NEUROPSYCHOLOGICAL DEFICITS IN THEIR CHILDREN.

ANOTHER INTERVENTION IS PARENT TRAINING: TEACHING PARENTS HOW TO APPROPRIATELY MODEL AND REINFORCE PROPER BEHAVIOR TO CHILDREN.

OH TONY, I KNOW THAT YOU ARE UPSET THAT WE WERE NOT ABLE TO SEE THE MONKEYS TODAY. BEING UPSET IS OKAY. WHY DON'T YOU TALK TO ME ABOUT HOW YOU FEEL?

ANOTHER WAY TO PREVENT THE DEVELOPMENT OF ANTISOCIAL BEHAVIOR IS TO IMPROVE CHILDREN'S' COGNITIVE DEVELOPMENT.

TONY! DID YOU BUILD THAT ALL BY YOURSELF? THAT IS FANTASTIC!

ULTIMATELY, THE GOAL OF THESE EARLY INTERVENTION PROGRAMS IS TO REDUCE THE RISK FACTORS FOR THE ONSET OF ANTISOCIAL BEHAVIOR AND TO INCREASE *PROTECTIVE FACTORS* THAT FOSTER RESILIENCE WHEN CONFRONTED WITH THESE RISK FACTORS.

THIS ISSUE EXPLORED THE ORIGINS OF DEVELOPMENTAL AND LIFE-COURSE THEORIES. THESE THEORIES TEND TO USE LONGITUDINAL RESEARCH TO DETECT CONTINUITY OR CHANGE OVER AN INDIVIDUAL'S LIFETIME. DEVELOPMENTAL THEORIES FOCUS ON A DEVELOPMENTAL PROCESS IN WHICH A PERSON PASSES THROUGH PREDICTABLE STAGES DURING HIS OR HER LIFETIME. LIFE-COURSE THEORIES, ON THE OTHER HAND, POSIT THAT BEHAVIOR IS NOT EASILY PREDICTED AND THAT UNPREDICTABLE EVENTS THAT OCCUR DURING THE LIFE COURSE MAY IMPACT WHETHER AN OFFENDER CHOOSES TO STOP COMMITTING CRIME. BOTH TYPES OF THEORIES FOCUS ON DETERMINING THE ONSET, PERSISTENCE, AND DESISTENCE OF OFFENDING, AS WELL AS THE PATHWAY OR SEQUENCE OF EVENTS THAT LEAD PEOPLE INTO AND OUT OF CRIME. ALTHOUGH ORIGINALLY DEVELOPED AS A CONTROL THEORY, MICHAEL GOTTFREDSON AND TRAVIS HIRSCHI'S SELF-CONTROL THEORY HAS BEEN PULLED INTO THE LIFE-COURSE PERSPECTIVE IN CRIMINOLOGY. THEY WERE TWO OF THE FIRST CRIMINOLOGISTS TO BEGIN TO EXAMINE CHILDHOOD AS AN IMPORTANT STAGE FOR THE ORIGIN OF OFFENDING BEHAVIOR. IN THEIR THEORY, THEY PROPOSE THAT SELF-CONTROL IS A CHARACTERISTIC THAT DEVELOPS DURING CHILDHOOD. IT IS THE RESTRAINT THAT ALLOWS PEOPLE TO RESIST CRIME AND OTHER SHORT-TERM GRATIFICATION. PEOPLE WITH LOW SELF-CONTROL TEND TO BE "IMPULSIVE, INSENSITIVE, PHYSICAL (AS OPPOSED TO MENTAL), RISK-TAKING, SHORT-SIGHTED, AND NON-VERBAL." LOW SELF-CONTROL IS THE RESULT OF INEFFECTIVE PARENTING AND THIS BECOMES STABILIZED BY THE TIME THE CHILD REACHES EIGHT YEARS OLD. THEREFORE, THE LEVEL OF SELF-CONTROL IS STABLE OVER THE LIFE COURSE, AFFECTING EVERY ASPECT OF A PERSON'S LIFE. THIS EXPLAINS CONTINUITY OF OFFENDING OVER THE LIFE COURSE.

TERRIE MOFFITT HAD ACCESS TO A VERY RICH LONGITUDINAL DATA SET COLLECTED DURING THE DUNEDIN MULTIDISCIPLINARY HEALTH AND DEVELOPMENT STUDY. IN ORDER TO EXPLAIN THE AGE-CRIME CURVE, SHE DEVELOPED HER DEVELOPMENTAL TAXONOMY (OR DUAL TAXONOMY THEORY) USING THE DUNEDIN STUDY DATA. SHE PROPOSED THAT THE AGE-CRIME CURVE CONSISTS OF TWO DISTINCT GROUPS OF OFFENDERS, LIFE-COURSE-PERSISTENT (LCP) OFFENDERS AND ADOLESCENCE-LIMITED (AL) OFFENDERS, AND THAT EACH HAD DIFFERENT ETIOLOGICAL REASONS FOR THEIR OFFENDING BEHAVIOR. LCP OFFENDERS BEGIN THEIR ANTISOCIAL BEHAVIOR AT AN EARLY AGE AND CONTINUE INTO ADULTHOOD. AL OFFENDERS' DELINQUENT BEHAVIOR IS LIMITED TO THEIR ADOLESCENT YEARS, AND THEY STOP WHEN THEY REACH ADULTHOOD. THIS EXPLAINS CONTINUITY OR CHANGE OF OFFENDING OVER THE LIFE COURSE.

ROBERT SAMPSON AND JOHN LAUB UNEXPECTEDLY DISCOVERED SHELDON AND ELEANOR GLUECKS' DATA THAT PROSPECTIVELY STUDIED 500 DELINQUENT BOYS AND 500 NON-DELINQUENT BOYS IN THE EARLY 20TH CENTURY. USING TRAVIS HIRSCHI'S SOCIAL BOND THEORY, THEY DEVELOPED THEIR AGE-GRADED THEORY OF INFORMAL SOCIAL CONTROL. THEY PROPOSED THAT SOCIAL BONDS ARE AGE-GRADED. THAT IS, SOCIAL BONDS VARY THROUGHOUT LIFE. IF BONDS TO VARIOUS INSTITUTIONS OF INFORMAL SOCIAL CONTROL, LIKE FAMILY OR SCHOOL, ARE WEAK, IT EXPLAINS CONTINUITY IN OFFENDING. HOWEVER, THEY ALSO BELIEVED THAT VARIOUS UNPREDICTABLE EVENTS CAN HAPPEN THAT MAY ALTER THE TRAJECTORY OF AN INDIVIDUAL'S LIFE, AND THESE TURNING POINTS CAN LEAD TO DESISTENCE FROM OFFENDING. THIS EXPLAINS CONTINUITY AND CHANGE OF OFFENDING OVER THE LIFE COURSE. BECAUSE THE FOCUS OF THESE THEORIES IS ON CHILDHOOD, POLICY IMPLICATIONS INCLUDE THE USE OF EARLY INTERVENTIONS SUCH AS PROPER PRENATAL CARE, AVOIDING BEHAVIORS THAT MAY JEOPARDIZE FETAL DEVELOPMENT, PARENT TRAINING, AND IMPROVEMENT OF THE COGNITIVE DEVELOPMENT OF CHILDREN.

GLUECK

Glueck

GLUECK

Key Terms

Cross-Sectional Research
Longitudinal Research
Developmental Theories
Life-Course Theories
Age-Crime Curve
Robert Sampson
Travis Hirschi
Sheldon and Eleanor Glueck
Risk Factors
Michael Gottfredson
John Laub
Terrie Moffitt
Phil Silva
Dunedin Multidisciplinary Health and Development Study
Self-Control Theory
Self-Control
Developmental Taxonomy
Dual Taxonomy Theory
Life-Course-Persistent (LCP)
Neuropsychological Deficits
Cumulative Continuity
Contemporary Continuity
Adolescence-Limited (AL)
Maturity Gap
Social Mimicry
Autonomy
Age-Graded Theory
Social Bond Theory
Turning Points
Human Agency
Early Intervention Programs
Protective Factors

Discussion Questions

1. Compare and contrast Gottfredson and Hirschi's self-control theory, Moffit's developmental taxonomy, and Sampson and Laub's age-graded theory. How does each theory account for continuity and/or change in their propositions?

2. What transitions or trajectories have you seen in your own life or your friends' lives that illustrate Sampson and Laub's age-graded theory? What events encouraged offending? What events discouraged it?

3. Given Moffitt's developmental taxonomy of life-course-persistent and adolescence-limited offenders, which should be given more attention in research and practice? Why do you believe this?

4. What risk factors might make someone more likely to engage in offending behavior? What protective factors might keep someone from engaging in offending behavior?

Suggested Readings

Gottfredson, M. R., & Hirschi, T. (1990). *A general theory of crime*. Stanford University Press.

Laub, J. H., & Sampson, R. J. (2003). *Shared beginnings: Divergent lives*. Harvard University Press.

Lilly, J. R., Cullen, F. T., & Ball, R. A. (2019). *Criminological theory: Contexts and consequences* (7th ed.). Sage Publications.

Moffitt, T. (1993). Adolescence-limited and life-course-persistent antisocial behavior: A developmental taxonomy. *Psychological Review, 100*, 674-701.

Sampson, R. J., & Laub, J. H. (1993). *Crime in the making: Pathways and turning points through life*. Harvard University Press.